SHALEEA VENNEY

With This Ring...

A 31 Day Devotional For Wives And Wives to Be.

Shaleea
VENNEY
AUTHOR SPEAKER MOTIVATOR

First edition

ISBN: 978-0-578-74340-0

This book was professionally typeset on Reedsy.
Find out more at reedsy.com

To My Sister In Christ,
Know that you are the prize. Know that you are worthy of true love.
God has heard you and will keep his promises to you. His timing is
perfect. I am praying for miracles, blessings, and abundance in
every area of your life. May God give you the desires of your heart.
May you only know Gods best!

Contents

Preface		iii
1	What Were You Expecting?	1
2	My Time, My Happiness	4
3	A Helpmate	6
4	It's What You Do	9
5	Going to Bed Angry	11
6	Talk That Talk...	14
7	To Submit?	18
8	Kindness Goes A Long Way	21
9	The Family that Prays	23
10	Complacency	25
11	Unpacking Our Sins	28
12	Not of this world?	31
13	When our Finances Are In Shambles.	34
14	Grief and Loss	37
15	Infidelity/Divorce	40
16	Overcoming Stress	44
17	What About Your Friends?	46
18	Thoughts of Sex	49
19	Loving Me For Me	52
20	Shhh!!!Just Tell God	55
21	I Don't Like Him...Sometimes!	58
22	God, Husband, Wife, Children	61
23	Lonely and Married	64
24	Choked By "What If"	67

25 God's Time   70
26 The Student   72
27 Pasts Can Sink The Future   75
28 Leave and Cleave   77
29 The Importance of Being Present   80
30 Forgiveness   83
31 That's Marriage   86
32 Your Notes And Thoughts....   88
About the Author   89

Preface

So many people want to have a wedding and wear the ring but they are not ready to be a wife. The fact that you are an adult who has fallen in love, has nothing to do with whether you will make a good wife or not. Statistics say that marriage is on the decline and that of those that do get married, more than 50% of them will end in divorce within the first 5 years. Why?

Have we become so self indulged and careless, that we no longer have what it takes to commit to the one person that we swore in front of God to love and cherish always? The idea of marriage is beautiful but, when you're actually in a marriage and realize that it is "real" and forever, tunes can change.

If you really want to be married, understand the seriousness of what you are saying. Are you ready to be selfless? Are you a helpmate? Can you take on someone else's baggage? Are you solid in who you are as a person and individual? You can't love someone else if you don't properly love yourself. You can't fill in your broken places by getting married and expect your husband to "fix" you. You must be a whole person going into marriage because marriage takes two whole people to work.

For richer or poorer. When you have an argument. When looks change. In sickness and in health. Through grief and mourning. For every good time. Through the worst of times. Through lies, broken trust, and every apology. On those days when you're not certain of anything- especially your marriage.

You can't just walk away. You don't get to just decide that due to a difference of opinion, you don't want to be married anymore. It's not like dating. You don't get to wake up and decide it's not working out and you'd like to swipe left! Nope! You are in it for the long haul.

Marriage is a daily commitment that two people must agree upon. Both parties must be willing participants. When the lust fades and the honeymoon phase is over, will your marriage still stand? Stop planning your wedding and focus on how to sustain a happy and healthy marriage. Life WILL happen to your marriage. How will you handle it? Are you ready?

1

What Were You Expecting?

So, you're ready to say "I do?" You've probably been daydreaming about this day your whole life and can't believe the time has finally come. You'll wear the perfect dress, and your hair and makeup will be flawless. Your maid of honor is already chosen. The venue is perfect….. Yep, everything is going to be perfect. You'll stand in front of your friends and family, marry the perfect man, have perfect children, and your life will be perfect.

You know where you want to live. You know what kind of car you want to drive and how many vacations you want to take a year. What will you do if life doesn't go the way you planned?

You chose to marry your husband because he's a solid man and he has a good heart. What will you do the first time he gets angry or stressed enough to lose his temper and yell at you? He has a great job so you know you'll be financially taken care of. What happens if he loses that big fancy job? What is your idea of a good husband? Hardworking, bill paying, charming, affectionate? What if he doesn't hug you enough? What happens when he doesn't talk to you the way you think he should? Does he have to open the door for you? Is it his job to pump the gas and change the oil?

What are you expecting? Your idea of marriage is based on your upbringing. Were you raised by a single parent? Have you ever seen what a healthy relationship looks like up close? Did your parents make their point by yelling at each other? Was your father a womanizer? Did he ever lay his hands on your mother? Was he there at all? What about your husbands' parents? What were they like? You are both coming in to this marriage with expectations based on your own life experiences. The same way you might be expecting him to change the engine oil and take out the trash, he might be expecting you to wash his clothes and be a great cook like his mother. What if you don't like to cook? What if he doesn't know anything about cars?

When we put our expectations of who we think people are supposed to be, above their realities, we cheat ourselves out of the opportunity to connect and to love unconditionally. This is also a recipe for disappointment. No one will live up to your expectations because people aren't meant to fit into a box. People thrive the most when they are loved for who they are unapologetically. No one should have to change to be "good enough" for you. People fall short and that is ok. There isn't a rule that decides who has to be what in your marriage as far as roles are concerned. Just be a team. He might be the better cook, you might be better at money management. Maybe he is better with children than you. We all have our strengths. Combine your strengths with his and be a power couple. You'll be much better off praising his strengths, than highlighting his weaknesses.

Let go of expectations of who you think he should be and get to know and love him for who he is. If you want to start your marriage on the right foot, start with a clean slate.

The Bible mentions love and breaks it down perfectly in **1 Corinthians 13:5 ESV** It does not insist on its own way; it is not irritable or resentful. Emphasis on: *It does NOT insist on its own way*. It can't be your way or no way.

Say this prayer:

Father God, as we embark on this journey together, help us both. We don't know what we are doing nor how to make this marriage work. We will need your insight and guidance. Help us to be slow to anger. Teach us to see one another for all of our good qualities and to be patient when we find things that aren't so flattering about each other. Remind us that we are both works in progress and that you are with us always. Let us always come to you for all matters concerning this union. In the mighty name of Jesus I pray, amen.

2

My Time, My Happiness

Why do you want to be married? Do you believe it will make you a better woman if someone calls you their wife? Do you believe society will view you differently if there's a ring on your left hand? Will it prove you're worthy? If you get married, will you be happy then? Are you happy now?

Understand one thing, being married will not make you happy. If you are not happy as an individual, you will not be happy as a wife. It is important to know who you are and what makes you happy. You need to be fulfilled and be passionate about something that is just for you-outside of a man. It could be music, arts, reading, writing, sports, working out, dance, travel, or something else. Only you know what it is for you. You need not lose your zest for life or your love for the things you are passionate about simply because you are married. If your only source of happiness comes from your marriage, you have an issue. Marriage isn't always blue skies and rainbows. What will you do to feed you spirit when you need a little "me time"?

"Me time" is imperative- even in the best marriages. You both need to be able to spend time apart refueling your happy tank from time to time. Don't feel guilty about this time, and don't neglect yourself or your need for a mental uplifting. Your mind, body, and spirit, needs to be full within your marriage and it's just as important to retain that same energy within yourself.

It is not your husbands responsibility to make you happy. If you are unhappy, it's your own fault- unless he is abusive, cruel, or the culprit (that's a different conversation). It is your responsibility to be paying attention to your "happy tank." When you see the low happiness indicator light turn on, you need to refuel. It doesn't even matter how well you're doing inside of your marriage. Your marriage could be thriving and you'd still need to carve out some space for "me time" because you need to be fulfilled outside of your union. "Me time" spent building yourself up, will also strengthen your marriage. It's a win win. When you are happy, you live and love better. A cheerful heart is good medicine, but a crushed spirit dries up the bones. **Proverbs 17:22 ESV.**

Say this prayer:

Lord, help me to not lose sight of my gifts and my joy just because I am married. Thank you for blessing me with a loving husband who will encourage me to care for myself and to do things that make me feel happy and whole. Help me to remember who I am in you. Let me always see life through childlike eyes so that I always have a passion for fun and living life with eyes wide open. Let me live life to the fullest and truly have it all. In the matchless name of Jesus I pray, amen.

3

A Helpmate

Help
Verb
"Make it easier for (someone) to do something by offering one's services or resources" **Mate**
Noun
"A person's husband, wife, or other sexual partner." **Merriam Webster**

Genesis 2:18–25: KJV "Then the LORD God said, 'It is not good that the man should be alone; I will make him a helper fit for him.' ... So the LORD God caused a deep sleep to fall upon the man, and while he slept took one of his ribs and closed up its place with flesh. And the rib that the LORD God had taken from the man he made into a woman and brought her to the man."

Marriage takes work and dedication but what does it mean to be a wife? You are a beautiful woman and your husband loves you, you'll make a great wife right? Not if that's all you have to bring to the table. Your beauty is wonderful but it should be a bonus, not your only quality. The dictionary describes **Help** as: Make it easier for (someone) to do something by offering one's services or resources. Sounds like in order to be a helpmate, there needs to be some helping.

Your husband needs a partner who can help him through life. When he is weak, you are strong. When his back itches, you scratch it. If he grills the meat, you prepare the side dishes. Don't misunderstand, he is also your other half as well. All that you are to him, he is to you. This is a partnership.

Life is better knowing that someone has your back, is there to catch you when you fall, and can help lighten the load. When life pushes you to the edge and the only thing that makes things ok, is the sound of their voice. It's anticipating one another's needs. Wiping tears when times get rough. Making a house into a home together. Raising children and growing old together. An entire life spent loving and caring for someone else.

Think about what kind of partner you are planning to be. What value do you bring to your husbands life? Do you have a solid plan? If you want to get married just to be a wife, then you shouldn't be getting married because when marriage gets real, you will not rise to the occasion. Go into your marriage with a service based mindset and find out how you can be of service to your husband and your children. You each have a role in your marriage.

Ecclesiastes 4:9-10 ESV "Two are better than one, because they have a good return for their labor: If either of them falls down, one can help the other up. But pity anyone who falls and has no one to help them up

Say this prayer:
Lord, help me to be the wife and helpmate you have called

for me to be. Let me be a blessing to my husband and everyone around us. It is my desire to be the greatest wife I can be and to make you proud. Let my husband truly find his "good thing" in me and obtain favor from you. Bless this union. Protect this union. Let us find our perfect match in one another. In the matchless name of Jesus I pray, amen.

4

It's What You Do

The trouble with the word love in this world we live in today is: it's too easily used. People often confuse lust with love. People often don't even know what the word means and how truly heavy the word is. Part of the reason for that is probably because most people are yearning for romantic love and want it so badly, they'll ignore the warning signs and whole heartedly run after the wrong person, only to find themselves hurt in the end. Love of course, is only elusive to those who confuse it at its simplest form. Love was never meant to be a noun, it is a verb.

1 Corinthians 13:4-5 NIV

"Love is patient, love is kind. It does not envy, it does not boast, it is not proud. It does not dishonor others, it is not self-seeking, it is not easily angered, it keeps no record of wrongs." If you are to adhere to the New Testament, "love" can never be merely a feeling or an emotion. It means taking actions that are not always beneficial to you. The word love without action, can not be "biblical love." Translation: Love is not what you say, it's what you do. Love without action is simply a well intended word.

Love is putting others before yourself. It's nurturing. It's apologizing when you were wrong and when you've offended. It's accepting apologies without reminding your partner of their wrongdoings. Love is doing things that you may not always feel like doing because it makes another person happy. It's giving without holding your generosity over someone's head. It's wiping sick noses, making soup, and making a conscious effort to show up for the person you love each day. Love is sacrifice. Love is work...if it's done right.

If you ever question someone's love for you, look at what they are willing to endure with you, or on your behalf and you'll answer your question. You have committed to someone in the highest way possible- marriage.

Understand that the wedding day is only one day, but the marriage has to be a daily priority for both of you, if it will succeed.

Say this prayer:

Father God, I ask that you bless this union. Teach us to be patient and kind to one another even when times are difficult. Fill our hearts with thanksgiving and gratitude and protect this union. In the name of Jesus I pray, amen.

5

Going to Bed Angry

Guess what? Sometimes marriage is hard. Anytime you take two adults, with different opinions, backgrounds, and thought processes and pair them together, you are bound to disagree on some things. Small disagreements can sometimes lead to big fights. As much as you love one another, an argument from time to time is inevitable. The goal is: If you have to fight, fight fair and smart. What does that mean? You know your spouses triggers and buttons. When is the best time to bring them up? During an argument because you want to hurt them for hurting you. Is that fair? Or, you're fighting about one thing and bring up a mistake they made years ago (which you've already forgiven them for) to add ammunition to your fire. Is that smart?

You feel like you are right and your spouse feels like they are right. Neither of you are even listening to one another because your sole focus is to be right. This will go nowhere quickly. You yell until you both get tired and go to bed with your backs facing one another or one of you may sleep on the couch. The next morning, you probably leave for work without saying goodbye.

11

What did you accomplish?

In **Ephesians 4:26-27** Paul says "In your anger do not sin": Do not let the sun go down while you are still angry, and do not give the devil a foothold. Paul is saying that sometimes we get angry and that's ok. What is NOT ok is how we handle our anger. Sometimes out of anger, we say and do things that we can't take back because we chose to be driven by our emotions. This opens the door for the devil to come in and wreak all sorts of havoc. We have no business speaking to anyone so callously, especially our spouses.

In marriage, it is imperative that you both realize that you are on the same team. You give strangers and colleagues the benefit of the doubt on a daily basis. Why aren't you able to afford your spouse the same mercy? Why can't you see your spouses good intentions? You know and married this person so why would you think that they'd intentionally hurt you?

Arguments are bound to happen but if you can't control your tongue, take a step back to breathe and then speak lovingly to your spouse. Leave the "You always" or the "Why would yous" behind. Ask yourself, is this thing that we are fighting about really this big of a deal? Whether it is or it isn't, approach your spouse from a place of love and compassion and he will soften his heart to you as well.

People have gotten divorced for some of the tiniest reasons because both partners refused to compromise or to be wrong. Most of those couples regret it. Do you want to be right, or do you want to be married?

Say this Prayer:
Father God, give me the patience and the strength to see the

good in my husband. Help me to hold my tongue when I want to spew angry words at him. Soften both of our hearts and help us to love and trust enough to be vulnerable with each other. Keep us bonded and in love. When we lose our way, guide us back. Wrap this union in your love, your mercy, and your grace Lord. In Jesus' name I pray, amen.

6

Talk That Talk...

Would you say that you communicate pretty well with your husband? Really? All the time? What about when you're upset? It matters how you speak to each other. It is important to set a standard for your communication style. Establish this early on. Perhaps you agree to not talk *at* each other. Maybe you don't want to scream. Maybe name calling is a "no no". You both know your deal breakers and if you don't, you better have a conversation.

There is beauty in being able to have an effective conversation. What is effective conversation? Effective conversation is being able to share your real feelings; good or bad, and feeling safe to do so. Have you ever wanted to tell someone how you *really* felt but felt like you couldn't because it would start an argument or they'd take it the wrong way, so you keep it to yourself only to later realize that it has morphed into resentment because you now feel like your feelings aren't valid?

The Bible says we are one flesh when we get married. The next time you get ready to have a conversation with your spouse, think about how YOU would like to be talked to. When you speak to your other half, you are speaking to yourself. Do you want to hurt him? You would never say cruel and hateful things to yourself would you? Don't you want him to listen to you when you you share your feelings? How would you feel if he interrupted you mid sentence? It'd be pretty obvious that he hadn't been listening at all and was only thinking of his next rebuttal while you were talking. **Proverbs 18:13 KJV** He that answereth a matter before he heareth *it*, it *is* folly and shame unto him. Not listening to your spouse is a recipe for disaster.

What are you saying to him? How are you saying it? Are you fighting fire with fire or are you trying to diffuse the situation. **Proverbs 15:1** A soft answer turns away wrath, but a harsh word stirs up anger. You know his buttons just as he knows yours. You know exactly how to turn the disagreement up a notch. What does that solve? Instead, be thoughtful and sincere in your responses. Don't be so quick to speak.

Whether you are laughing or going through a bump in your marriage, gentleness certainly goes a long way. Communication in marriage is not difficult at all if you learn to communicate from the heart. There is a great tool that some therapists use to help couples break the ice and learn to communicate by seeing one another's point of view. You each sit across from one another and you focus on your spouses concerns by starting off your sentence with "If you really knew me you'd know" followed by whatever they're upset about. For example. "If you really knew me, you'd know that when I said we could spend more time together, I meant it with all my heart. I would never want to intentionally hurt you or make you feel that you're not my priority because you are. I'm so sorry I have been so busy with work." You state the issue and sincerely state your truth from the heart. Then, your spouse replies. For example: "If you really knew me, you'd know that I am not upset about you working long hours. I know you are doing it to make sure we are taken care of and I appreciate all that you do. I just miss you and need some quality time with you." Now both parties have heard and understand the other because they have spoken their truths with gentleness, kindness, and sincerity. You have both been forced to only speak on the issue at hand and not talk around the issue or bring up other things. It is very hard to be upset with someone you love when you learn to soften your hearts, stare into their eyes, and give them your undivided attention.

When you have moments when you can't sit down and have those face to face conversations, do it by yourself and see if doesn't help your anger to dissipate. Think about your husband and his heart. Did he really want to yell at this morning when he left for work, or was he just tired and took it out on you? Did you really mean to be rude earlier when he called you or, were you just frustrated because the dog just used the bathroom in the house and the baby was crying? Marriage is about *really* knowing someone and their true intentions. When you build a bond and solid foundation, you won't let little things turn into big issues anymore because you both are looking for the best in each other. Try it now. Did your husband mean it how you heard it? Was he really trying to upset you? Did you mean for what you said to come out the way it sounded? Facial expression and all? Take the time to communicate properly and sincerely and you will be just fine. Sorry is not a bad word. It doesn't mean you've done anything wrong, sometimes, it means I'm sorry if it came out that way. It's letting your spouse know that he means more to you than a misunderstanding. Life is too short. Try to spend it with as many happy moments as possible.

James 1:19 ESV Know this, my beloved brothers: let every person be quick to hear, slow to speak, and slow to anger.

Say this Prayer:

Father God, help me to tame my mouth and my facial expressions-(you know me Lord!). Show me how to communicate effectively and gingerly. Please don't ever let me forget why I fell in love with this man and allow me to see him through your eyes when my vision gets cloudy. I know that you have sent us to each other for a reason and I thank you for blessing me with someone to enjoy life with. Let us be quick to hear, slow to speak, and slow to anger. Let us be quick to forgive and to be full of understanding and patience. Lord I ask you to surround us with your blood and mercy. In Jesus' name I pray, amen.

7

To Submit?

submit

Verb.
To yield oneself to the authority or will of another : Surrender-
Merriam Webster.

Let's talk about submission. There has been lots of talk about the S word and how to apply it in our everyday lives. Women are more educated and capable today than ever before. Should you be submitting to your men? Some people feel that this part of the Bible is outdated and that there's no place for submission in today's society.

Ephesians 5:21 ESV: Says "Submit to one another out of reverence for Christ."

22 Wives, submit to your own husbands, as to the Lord. **23** For the husband is the head of the wife even as Christ is the head of the church, his body, and is himself its Savior. **24** Now as the church submits to Christ, so also wives should submit in everything to their husbands. **25** Husbands, love your wives, as Christ loved the church and gave himself up for her.

It's really a matter of your interpretation. The Bible speaks about submitting to *one another.* Your husband is the head of the family but, that by no means diminishes your gifts and abilities. He should consult you when he is making decisions, and solicit your advice. A partnership in its finest form. He should submit to you as well. He will love and honor you as Christ loved the Church. He is to love you as he loves himself. (**Ephesians 5:33 ESV** However, let each one of you love his wife as himself, and let the wife see that she respects her husband.) Your husband should have a heart to hear from God because if God leads him, he will then lead the family with love.

Even societal norms tell us that our men are supposed to be able to provide for our families, pay bills, and cover/protect our households. Many women have turned potential suitors away and said no to dates because the man wasn't of a certain financial status, or she didn't feel "safe" in his presence. The question is: Why do so many people have an issue with the idea of submission, when society has taught us from the beginning that the man is supposed to be the man of the house?

Merriam Webster defines Submit as a verb meaning: To yield oneself to the authority or will of another : Surrender. How lovely would it be to surrender to the person you love? When you think of surrender, what comes to mind? Utter trust? Vulnerability? Peace? It is not wise to submit to just anyone but if you are going to submit, why not submit to your husband? You have chosen him wisely right? Do you trust his judgment? Does he make you feel safe and help take the load off your shoulders? Does he care about the things that matter to you? Does he have both of your best interests in the forefront of his mind? Couldn't you breathe a sigh of relief when you answer those questions with a yes?!

Submission isn't about becoming a doormat or acquiescing to his whims. Submission, doesn't mean that you become small and allow your husband to completely envelop you in a shroud of arrogance or misplaced leadership. Submission means trusting the man you married to be sensitive to your needs, and respectfully honor your opinions. It means that he is trustworthy enough to hear a word from God and lead by example. It is your duty as a Christian wife, to allow your man to lead your family.

Your man is the head of the household because he has earned his role and if he is not a good steward over your family, he will have to one day look God in the eye and explain himself.

Say this Prayer:
Father God, help me to take my pride out of this marriage and to trust the man that you have blessed me with to lead this family. Lord let me be his shoulder when he is weak, and be his partner when he makes decisions. Help him to honor and love me as you love the church. Let us have equal respect for each other and let us see each other through your eyes. Help our love to grow stronger each day. Above all, let the both of us continue to submit to you and to never lose sight of the fact that you are the head of our lives. In the matchless name of Jesus I pray, amen.

8

Kindness Goes A Long Way

Lots of people say that kindness and chivalry have died in the world. This isn't really true if we're being completely honest. Most people are still pretty kind and courteous. Haven't you held the door for a stranger, said "thank you" when you were helped by servers, let someone cut ahead of you in traffic? Don't you still say "excuse me" when you need to get by someone, or "sorry" when you've offended? No! The world hasn't lost it's kindness, our homes have. We are so busy out here trying to prove to strangers that our mothers raised us right, that we kick our shoes off and let our rude hair hang down at home.

Have you ever noticed that we typically treat strangers with more respect and kindness than our spouses and families? Here's the kicker: your spouse enjoys a simple "thank you" just as much as the next person. Kindness goes a long way in every area of our lives, but this is especially true in your marriage. One of the biggest complaints married couples have is "He or she takes the little things I do for granted" We all do things for our spouses and our children without ever hearing as much as a thank you. Women constantly say motherhood is a thankless job. Does it really have to be? Can we not change the narrative in our homes to appreciation and gratitude? Things would change for the better if we started acknowledging the nice things we do for one another and holding the doors for each other at home, even when we believe our partners are fully capable of doing so. We all want to feel appreciated, your spouse is no different. We often get so caught up in the idea of "Well, he's supposed to do this or that because he's my husband," that we fail to realize that even our spouses don't "owe" us. Appreciation should be a given. The Bible reminds us of how we should treat each other in Ephesians.

Ephesians 4:2 KJV : With all lowliness and meekness, with longsuffering, forbearing one another in love.

Good manners matter and never go out of style. Be sure to treat your husband with the same kindness you give to strangers... Gratitude will keep your bond strong.

Say this Prayer,

Father God, please teach me to be patient, kind, and generous to the love that you have given to me. Help me to be a good steward over his heart and his feelings. Let him wake up each day with a heart full of love and happiness. Bless me to wake up with that same happiness in my heart as well. Let us be passionate lovers, the closest of friends, and wrapped under your guidance as long as we both shall live. In Jesus' name I pray, amen.

9

The Family that Prays

You must assure that your family is covered under the word of God. With your husband as the head of the family, the two of you must work diligently to assure your children have a relationship with the Lord. Teach them to pray early. Let your children see you both praying together. Let your children see you worship. They need to see prayer and worship regularly so that they are not ashamed of either activity and can learn both for themselves. Your children need to see you both turn to God when times are good and when times are bad. From simple things like blessing the food, to more challenging times like praying over a sick loved one.

Proverbs 22:6 KJV reminds us to: Train up a child in the way he should go; even when he is old he will not depart from it. You must train up your children with this solid foundation because even when life happens and they lose their way, they will always come back to the basics. The greatest thing you can teach your children is love for God. Attend church as a family unit.

Be proud of your love for God. Have family bible study in

your home. Teach your children to say their prayers at bedtime. Pray with and for your children when they become unruly. Pray with and for your husband daily. Pray for your husband when he is having a bad day and doesn't have the strength to pray for himself. Sharing your love for God with each other will deepen your bond. The world says to love your spouse but, the Holy Spirit will teach you how. God's love is the best love. Relish in it. There is power in a praying wife and mother. Go to God with all of your concerns, joys and thanksgiving. No matter what is going on around you, stand in the word of God and have faith in it.

Joshua 24:15 But as for me and my household, we will serve the Lord.

Don't be afraid to get on your knees and fall on your face on behalf of your family. Keep God first. Don't underestimate the power of faith and prayer. Prayer changes everything. Prayer keeps families together and strong.

Say this prayer:
Father God, I ask that you be a blanket of protection around my family. Cover us. Guide our steps and help us to navigate the ills of this world in a way that is pleasing to you. Lord, let this family be a shining example of your light for others. Bless us in every arena of our lives- mentally, physically, relationally, and financially. Keep us grounded. Continue to give us favor. We thank you for all that you have done and everything you will continue to do for this family. In Jesus' name I pray, amen.

10

Complacency

Complacency is a marriage's worst enemy. When we are dating, we do everything we can to make our husbands fall in love with us. Wearing our hair a certain way, wearing certain shoes and nice dresses. We try to woo him with our cooking skills and to impress him with our special talents. We do all of this so that our men can see without a doubt; *here is your dream girl*. He sees it and because he is an intelligent man, he marries you. Mission accomplished! Both of you plan on living happily ever after.

Life happens very quickly and things can change even quicker. Both of you start working on your careers and trying to climb the ever evolving corporate ladder. You buy a home. You have children. Life keeps coming. Somewhere along the way, you lose sight of one another, even if it's not intentional. In life, whatever you concentrate on the most will flourish. When one thing thrives, another one will suffer. Your relationship can never be what suffers.

All of a sudden, date nights are far and few in between and, the baby gets all of the romantic evenings that used to belong to the two of you. Passionate nights are replaced with much needed rest because you're both exhausted. You begin to see each other less and less as the exciting and impassioned lovers that you once were, and more as partners/roomates. Sex is more and more infrequent. How does it ever get this far? How do you fix it?

No matter what happens, you mustn't ever forget to "love on your spouse". Text messages throughout the day when you can't call, just letting them know they're on your mind. "Just because" gifts. Wearing those cute heels he likes and your hair the way he likes. Date nights are important! Even if it's a candle lit dinner at home. Your relationship takes work to maintain. All those things you did in the beginning need to be kept up.

Work on yourself so that you're always interesting and growing. Don't let yourself go. Weight gain will happen especially with age and hormonal changes, but try to remain the woman that he fell in love with as much as possible. As much as society hates to admit it, looks matter. There's nothing wrong with your husband wanting you to remain the woman he fell in love with or you wanting to stay attracted to your husband. It takes work on both sides to show up each day for each other. Of course, neither of you are here based solely on attraction, but being attracted to every part of your spouse is beautiful.

You mustn't forget why you fell in love and hold onto that. Just because you're married to each other doesn't mean you get to check out. You don't get married and think "I have him now, so I don't need to try anymore". Quite the contrary, you cannot afford to stop showing up in your marriage. Don't take your spouse for granted. You should each make the effort to put one another first.

A sweet reminder that marriage and relationships take work,

can be found in Genesis.

"And Jacob served seven years for Rachel; and they seemed unto him but a few days, for the love he had to her." **Genesis 29:20.** During those times, daughters were also objects of value for their families. Jacob spoke to Laban about the affection he had for his daughter Rachel. Because he had nothing of value to offer to Laban for her hand in marriage, he promised seven years of service instead. His love for her was so great that he was willing to work for her. His work began long before the wedding, and he was happy to do it. Because he knew he was working for the woman he loved, time just flew by because he knew he was working for the ultimate prize. Let us stay committed to doing the work in our relationships.

Say This Prayer:
Father, thank you for blessing me with a loving husband. Help us to not become distracted and to keep this relationship and family a priority. Help us to love each other with your best love. When we have bad days and or lose our way, guide us back to one another and back to you Lord. Help us to always be attracted to each other. Bless this union. Let no works of the enemy come against it. In Jesus' name I pray, amen.

11

Unpacking Our Sins

You are two people learning about one another. You both have a story. You have both done and seen things that you may not be proud of. It is possible that you may be further along in your walk with the Lord than your spouse is. He may have some habits that he hasn't yet gotten under control. You will need to tread lightly and remember one thing: YOU have also fallen short of the glory of the Lord. You have also done things that weren't pleasing to the Lord.

Luke 6:37 KJV Do not judge, and you will not be judged. Do not condemn, and you will not be condemned. Forgive, and you will be forgiven

Do not judge your husband because he still falls short. Of course, there are limits to this. If he is out murdering people for fun, this is probably a deal breaker :-) but, if the offense is fixable, you can work with him. People are set in their ways. Some people don't see anything wrong with their way of life. Some people may not even realize they are doing the thing that bothers you. Open communication is the key. You can't just expect your spouse to read your mind and automatically know that his bad habits bother you. That's not fair to either of you. This is your friend and partner. You should be able to be honest with him and he should be able to hear you out.

You must set the tone early and often by expressing your feelings in a non judgmental way. Don't corner your partner and speak hastily or angrily. Speak lovingly to him. Don't use accusatory tones. Allow your partner the time to correct their behavior. Habits are hard to break. It's not easy to change. When you've done all you can do and you feel yourself getting frustrated, think about your past. You weren't always perfect. You know what it is like to struggle with shortcomings. Lean into your partner with that understanding.

There is power in a praying wife. Sometimes our struggles are bigger than the both of us. Sometimes, only God can create a change in a persons heart. Don't be afraid to cry out to God with your husband and on his behalf. God knows how to go directly to his heart and make him brand new. It's not your job to "fix" your husband, it's God's. Your job is to stand with him and pray for him. Your job is to make sure he knows he is loved and safe with you.

Anytime you merge two lives there will be growing pains. It's not easy. You are not perfect. He is not perfect. You must be ok with that. Contrary to what the world will have you to believe, people *can* change. You must love your spouse despite their imperfections just as God loves us all.

Say This Prayer,
Father, help me to love my husband and focus more on his goodness. I know that you are God and that you alone have the power to change him. I call on you right now father God and I ask that whatever we are doing that is not pleasing to you, be

taken out of our hearts right now God. Restore our focus. Give us minds to be more like you in every way. Let our love grow stronger for each other each day and thank you for being the third person in this marriage. Build us up Lord. I magnify your name and give you total control over this household. In Jesus' name I pray, amen.

12

Not of this world?

Relationship goals? Couple goals? Do it for the gram? Be careful what you let the world teach you about love and life. There is more to life than cars, money, houses, and "turning up" with your man. The world has a very skewed idea of what love is and if you start basing your love off of what you see other couples doing on social media, your marriage could be doomed.

1 John 2:16 KJV For all that *is* in the world—the lust of the flesh, the lust of the eyes, and the pride of life, is not of the Father but is of the world.

The world offers only a craving for physical pleasure, a craving for everything we see, and pride in our accomplishments and worldly possessions. The Bible teaches us that it is the things we see that are *not* real. Never covet anyone else's relationship or life for that matter. There is no need to keep up with the Joneses. You are not missing out on anything. The Joneses will have you in divorce court.

Instead, you must focus on building a solid foundation with your husband. Crave his presence. Yearn for his laugh. You should desire to become one flesh with your husband. Being

31

the best of friends will ensure an unbreakable bond. *THAT* is relationship goals. It's a closeness that doesn't always need to be captured on social media because it is best lived out loud in moments of bliss with your sweetheart.

There is a reason that they tell you that lots of couples break up after they go "public" on social media. Is social media killing love? No! Social media is simply distorting your idea of what real love looks like. Social media allows others to make uninformed assumptions about your life based on a pic that captured one iota of your life. People see this little snippet of your life, heavily read into it and, think they've got the relationship all figured out. Seeing beautiful people on your phone portray lust and call it love, can lead you to believe that your relationship is missing something or that your love life isn't as solid and exciting as theirs. Don't be so busy trying to prove your love to the world that you forget to prove it to each other-in private. Everything simply isn't for everyone. If there's any part of life that you keep for yourself, let your marriage be it. Focus on making one another happy. Focus on making one another feel safe. Learn to communicate with purpose. Find true happiness at home first.

Social media is full of distractions and temptation and has been the downfall to countless relationships. Everyone has been tempted to click on certain viral images, and to slide into a dm or to respond once someone has slid into your dm. Don't fall into these traps. Block out unnecessary distractions. If your timeline/feed doesn't inspire you, challenge you, and make you reach higher, you need to do a social media cleanse. The images you are seeing all day have a huge affect on your thought process and your relationship. The smallest thoughts can mature into big mistakes. You must be careful and cover your relationship with the Lords armor at all times.

Your marriage *is* relationship goals. It can be the best marriage in the world if you want it to be. You must water it and tend to it if you want it to be healthy. Comparison is a toxic weed in your garden of love, it only kills what your love could blossom into. Don't do it. Don't compare your house, your spouse, your car, or your bank accounts with anyone else's. Be happy with where you are. People show you their wins and triumphs without mentioning their tears and losses. Don't be fooled. Everything isn't what it seems. Remain grounded, humble, and prayerful.

Say this Prayer:

Father God, give me an eye to focus on what really matters. For I know that you have blessed us and that you have more blessings coming our way. Please help us to have eyes only for one another even when we are faced with temptation. Strengthen our friendship, and our bond. Let us find rest in each other's arms. Give us hearts of gratefulness and thanksgiving. Allow us to never forget how blessed we are to have found each other and never to take each other for granted. God, never let us stray from you or each other. In the mighty name of Jesus I pray, amen.

13

When our Finances Are In Shambles.

For better or for worse. Right? In sickness and in health. Correct? For richer or for poorer...HOLD ON! WHAT?! For richer is a breeze. What happens when we have to exercise the "for poorer" part of our vows? Job loss, bills and tribulation will happen to us all. What is one of the biggest reasons couples fight and or divorce? You guessed it! Money! Can your marriage withstand financial woes?

Matthew 6:25 KJV "Therefore I say to you, do not worry about your life, what you will eat or what you will drink; nor about your body, what you will put on. Is not life more than food and the body more than clothing?

God says we shouldn't worry about our lives. Matthew 6:25 is great in theory but, how practical is this scripture when you have an eviction notice? What about when your car's about to be repossessed and your husband is between jobs? Are we still supposed to be not worrying about our lives Matthew? Needless to say, this is much easier said than done. Or is it?

Trials and tribulation will happen to you at some point in your relationship. Even the wealthiest people are not immune to money issues. Finances are no different than any other area of a believer's life. We are called to pray and talk to God about all things that concern us-even money. God wants us to trust him as our source in this world. Those times when your bills are due and you have no idea how you'll make it through, yet time after time, you come out on the other side the victor? God. When you struggled to find food to eat, and someone bought you lunch? God. How bout when you're down to your last and out of nowhere, the situation worked out in your favor? Yep! God did it every time! He will do it every time.

Thank God for bringing you through. Learn to manage your money as best as you can. Give cheerfully (**2 Corinthians 9:6-8**) to others and in your tithes and offerings. When you build a solid relationship with money, and show the Lord that you can be trusted with money, he will increase your territory by blessing you with more. No matter how hard the times are that you're currently facing, God has not forgotten you and is with you. Don't lose faith and stand firm together on the word of God. He will see you through and you're going to have a testimony.

Say this Prayer:
Father God, I thank you. I thank you for every blessing. For our health, for each meal, for the lights, for gas in the car. Thank you for waking me up this morning. Thank you for the shelter over our heads and for loving us. I thank you for more than enough. Thank you for letting us be a blessing to someone else. For putting us into a position to lend and not borrow. God thank you for seeing us through every trial. You are an awesome God. Please continue to let your light shine on us and guide us in everything we do. In the mighty name of Jesus I

pray, amen.

14

Grief and Loss

Through sickness and in health. For richer or for poorer. Good times and bad. Through grief and loss. There will come a time when you feel the sting of a loss of someone close to you or your husband. You will have the wind knocked out of you at the news and you will feel like your world has shattered. It can be even harder when it is your husbands loved one who has gone on to be with the Lord. You may not have ever seen your husband so distraught or really cry his eyes out before. His brokenness can be enough to tear your heart in two too.

Parents, grandparents, siblings, close friends, and heaven forbid-your children may be suddenly taken away from you at any time. Death is a part of life and grief is apart of the human experience. It is normal and natural. When you are sitting in the middle of your grief and it feels as though it has overtaken you, remember that "Weeping may endure for a night, but joy comes in the morning" **Psalm 30:5 KJV**. Rest in the fact that your grief is needed. Sometimes it can even cause you to shift your mindset and have a spiritual awakening. Grief always has a purpose even if it's just closure. It won't last always.

Although you may be feeling like you have the weight of the world on your shoulders, you are not alone. God is with you. One of the best ways to deal with your hurt is to give it to God. Casting all your cares on Him, because he cares for you. **1 Peter 5:7.** There is no need to suffer in silence alone. God can hear your cries and He will wipe your tears if you invite him into your life during this difficult time. Don't shut out God and don't shut out your loved ones. You don't need to be strong alone. Let others be there for you. God calls us to support our brothers and sisters by grieving with those who are grieving. Rejoice with those who rejoice, weep with those who weep. **Romans 12:15 ESV**

To be absent from the body is to be present with the Lord **2 Corinthians 5:8 ESV.** Be a support system if your spouse is experiencing the loss of someone in his life. If you are experiencing loss, lean on your husband, God, and your support system and know that this pain too shall pass. God is listening and is with you through it all. He is always there for the brokenhearted. You can handle this.

Say this Prayer:

Father God, We are dealing with a huge loss and we are hurting. Lord give us peace during this trying time. Give us comfort and touch our hearts. Lord, this is a pain that only you can heal and we need you to intervene. We won't question you, we will only thank you. Thank you for bringing our loved one home and welcoming them through the gates. There is no more suffering for them in this world and we are thankful Lord. Lord, heal our hearts and the hearts of all of those our loved one left behind here on earth. We rest in the fact that we will see our loved one again one day in heaven so we thank you Lord.

Surround us with a peace that surpasses our understanding. In Jesus' precious name I pray, amen.

15

Infidelity/Divorce

What do you do when you find out that your happily ever after is not what you thought it was? How do you react when your beating heart is pulled from your chest and the pain is so unimaginable you can hardly breathe? Your mind is racing with thoughts and questions as you try to put the puzzle together in your mind. How could this happen? How could he cheat? What now? Should you get divorced?

The worst pain in the world is the one that comes from being hurt by the person in the world that you are *closest* to. When the person who has vowed to love and honor you in front of God reneges on that promise, it can tear your heart apart. Then, there's the confusion and the insecurity-wondering "Why wasn't I enough?" Although this man has hurt you to your core and you are angry at him, you still love him. You still love him and it makes you feel pathetic and stupid. You're not.

At this point you have two options: Stay or let it go. But what does God say about divorce? **Malachi 2:16 KJV** "For I hate divorce!" says the LORD, the God of Israel. "To divorce your wife is to overwhelm her with cruelty," says the LORD of

Heaven's Armies. "So guard your heart; do not be unfaithful to your wife." **Matthew 5:32 KJV** But I say to you that everyone who divorces his wife, except on the ground of sexual immorality, makes her commit adultery, and whoever marries a divorced woman commits adultery. Welp, you could walk away from him and you'd be totally within your rights as a woman of God. The Bible clearly states that infidelity is a deal breaker and grounds for divorce. But, are you sure that you want to get divorced?

This is not the time to make hasty decisions based on how you feel or due to fear of what people will think about you. The best thing to do is to get quiet so that you can hear from God. Cry, and then cry out to God. Don't talk to any of your negative/messy friends and family about the situation because they will most likely try to sway your decision based on their own fears and limited view points. Seek only the church and or your spiritual guides at this time. It's best to keep this situation to yourself so that when you make a decision, it is yours alone. The less others know, the less they have to talk about later. If you decide to stay with your husband and your loved ones know that he cheated, even though you've forgiven him, they may not. They may hold it over his head for years to come. It's not good. Everyone doesn't need a front row ticket to your marriage and everyone's advice shouldn't be solicited.

A wise Pastor I know once said "Although divorce because of sexual immorality is an option, it's not God's ideal situation. God can heal anything, but it will take work on both of your parts. If he expresses true regret, remorse, and contrition and, does the necessary work and it's visible before you, you have made the right decision by fighting for your marriage".

If your husband made a mistake, is truly sorry, and shows

you that he wants to heal the damage he has caused, then your marriage might be worth saving. Only you know that. You *know* your husband and his heart. You know if he has changed or if he is simply telling you what he thinks you need to hear. Pray and talk to God and do not be cruel to your husband while you sort out your feelings. There is no sense in trying to make him hurt as much as you do. When a man loves *truly* a woman, if she is hurt, it also hurts him. The thoughts of uncertainty and whether you'll stay with him, will be hurtful enough for him. Do not keep reminding him of what he has done, he remembers. Bringing it up does more damage than good.

Your marriage can overcome infidelity and broken trust. IF your husband has learned from his mistake and does the work to rebuild the love and trust, your marriage can be stronger than ever when you get to the other side of infidelity. We are only human, we make mistakes. Yes infidelity can be a deal breaker but it doesn't *have* to be. Only you know what is right for you and your family.

"Haven't you read that at the beginning, the Creator 'made them male and female,' and said, "For this reason, a man will leave his father and mother and be united to his wife, and the two will become one flesh?" So they are no longer two but one. Therefore what God has joined together, let man not separate" **Matthew 19:4-6 KJV**.

Say this Prayer,

Father God, I stand before you with my broken heart open and in need of your guidance. God, strengthen my heart. You see the hurt and pain that I am feeling right now and I ask that you give me peace during this difficult time. I speak to the very heart of my husband right now Lord. Lord give him a mind to focus on your word. Grow him into the man that you have called him to be. When he is distracted with ungodly thoughts, speak to him Lord and help him to renew his mind each day. Give him the desire to be better. Lord please soften my heart so that I am able to see clearly and so that I do not lash out at him when I am having moments of uncertainty. Help me to not hold grudges and to truly forgive him. Surround this marriage with your grace and mercy right now. I pray your will over us Lord. In Jesus' name I pray, amen.

16

Overcoming Stress

Meditate
Verb
to focus one's thoughts on : reflect on or ponder over-
Merriam Webster

That stress doesn't look very good on you. You may have been hit with some bad news. Perhaps one or both of you has lost their job. Maybe you can't make ends meet. You could be dealing with an illness or unexpected loss. It's a rough time and you are so afraid that things will not be ok. So far, you've just been making it little by little but you're not sure how much longer you can live like this. You've been praying but it seems like it's been on deaf ears because nothing has changed. You're not sure what you're going to do. HAVE FAITH.

Corinthians 5:7 KJV For we walk by faith, not by sight." You have to be careful not to base your views off of what you see. The things that you see are temporary and fleeting. You must trust the Lord with all your heart and believe that He will see you through any obstacles you face. Have faith that things will work out and they will. No matter what it looks like around you, stand firm on your faith. Be working in the natural realm to find a solution and trust God in the spiritual realm to send reenforcement on your behalf. You must do your part while God does His. Your outlook has everything to do with your ability to overcome.

He is working behind the scenes on your behalf. He is making a way out of no way. Press on and don't give up now. God is able to change your circumstances in a minute. He has not forgotten you, He will not leave nor forsake you. **Matthew 6:34 KJV** Therefore, do not worry about tomorrow, for tomorrow will worry about its own things. Sufficient for the day *is* its own trouble. - Don't worry about anything; instead, pray about everything. Tell God what you need, and thank him for all He has done. Remember this: You can focus on the problem *or* the praise but, it can't be both simultaneously. Whatever you give the most attention to will blossom and keep getting bigger. Make sure it's your praise being magnified.

Say this Prayer:

Father God, you see the situation and I am asking for your help. I know you see the need and that you are able to work this out for my good. I need a miracle Lord. Please help me to find some peace during this difficult time. My mind is so loud and crowded with thoughts of despair because I am worried when I know I should be trusting you. Forgive me Father. Help me Lord. Help me to trust you and to be quiet. I give my burdens to you simply because this is your battle. Thank you for stepping in on my behalf. I believe everything you said in your word and I can now rest in perfect peace. I believe it is already done. In Jesus' name I pray, amen.

17

What About Your Friends?

How's your sister circle? The company you keep can make or break you. What are their intentions? Are they grounded in their faith or their flesh? You must be selective with whom you share yourself with and, friends are no different. Friendship takes energy and effort to be successful. It's a commitment. Be careful who you choose to call a friend. People will always show their true intentions at some point, don't overlook the little things, or think they "didn't mean it how it sounded." People know what they are doing and what they are saying. Everyone doesn't have to be close to you. You must be guarded about who you allow into your inner circle. Everyone can't have access to you- that is reserved for the best.

1 Corinthians 15:33 ESV Do not be deceived: "Bad company ruins good morals." The Bible is clear about the spiritual risks we take when we associate with those who are out of touch with God." You see it everyday in the world we live in. Slowly but surely, things that are bad from a biblical standpoint are becoming normalized so much so, that even some believers are becoming desensitized to what they are seeing. You are not allowed to go against the grain and speak against things that you believe to be wrong because of your faith, out of fear of offending someone. This is also true with friendships. People crave friendships so much that they often overlook their own morals and values just to feel included.

Some people feel that they must stick to people they've known for a long time simply because they've known them for a long time. Some of these relationships are rooted in trauma. Perhaps you got close after a tragedy, or you have something in common that bonded you for longer then it should have. Trauma bonds are especially dangerous because they are not built on a solid foundation. The emotions that trauma creates can feel like forever bonds, but there is no bond, and it was never supposed to be a long term relationship. You were supposed to learn, grow, and keep going. Time has no weight on a friendship. Sometimes the people you have known the longest, can be your biggest downfall because they've known you since "way back when." This poses a problem because they often want to remember you the way they met you, and your growth comes across to them as "acting brand new/ acting funny." Run! These are not your friends.

Don't ever shrink yourself to be friends. Not every acquaintance you meet is meant to be rooted in your life permanently. You're not meant to hold onto everyone. Some come to teach you a lesson, some come to enable you to be a blessing, some come to be a blessing, and some come seeking you as an opportunity-as in, they think you can do something for them. They will all look the same initially. You need Gods discernment to help you to know the difference.

You know right away when a friendship is meant to be and you can tell when the chemistry is being forced. Don't force it.

You need friendships that pour into you.Your friends should build you up and make you dream bigger. Your friends should be rooting for you to win and willing to help you to get to the next level. They are not jealous of your successes and don't feel as though you are bragging when you discuss your wins or dreams with them. They are willing participants in your life and will show up for you time and time again. They are more like chosen family. **Proverbs 18:24 ESV** A man of many companions may come to ruin, but there is a friend who sticks closer than a brother. You need these people.

Say this Prayer:

Father God, give me the discernment to see through your eyes. If someone is not for me and doesn't want the best for me, remove them from my life. Lord, bless them, lift them up, and give them a heart to love. Send me a tribe that wants what's best for me and will pray for me and my family. Let us be close like family and be a blessing to one another. Surround me with peace and love. In Jesus' name I pray, amen.

18

Thoughts of Sex

The world has placed a huge emphasis on sex. It now seems that sex is worshipped on the level that God should be. You can't turn on the tv, pick up your phone, or turn on the radio without being reminded that YOU need to be sexier and that there are women all over the place ready to jump into bed with your husband. It can be exhausting and disheartening. You start looking at social media posts more closely because you heard about a viral video of a young woman doing something on camera. You read comments and see how men fall all over these types of women. You see perfectly purchased bodies that look nothing like yours. You begin to feel insecure. You wonder if your husband secretly wants a girl like that. If he too is seeing these videos or lusting after these women behind closed doors. He is a man after all. You begin to wonder if you are enough anymore. Could she do something for your husband that you can't? Could he? Would he cheat on you? You find yourself "peeking" at certain web pages, or certain "model" pages. You're mostly there taking mental notes and looking for ways to spice things up at home, perhaps to learn a trick or two to keep your man interested. Nothing wrong with this right? Well……

Thoughts lead to suggestions and suggestions lead to actions. You must be careful what you allow into your spirit. It's not as innocent as you think it is. You are unknowingly opening a can of worms. How many videos will you watch? How much of what these young women are doing is ok? How much of it are you going to bring back into your marriage? Are you lusting after some of these women now as well. Are you getting turned on? Be honest, there's no one else here.

When you allow certain images and fantasies into your spirit, they leave a stain on the fiber of your moral compass. There are many Christians addicted to porn. Porn isn't a realistic depiction of lovemaking and it is meant to be a fairy tale for adults. It's well shot and rehearsed. Real life often doesn't look anything like it, and when it doesn't, you or your spouse may be left feeling like something is missing. Some people even fantasize about other people when they are with their spouse.

1 Corinthians 6:18 KJV "Flee from sexual immorality. Every other sin a person commits is outside the body, but the sexually immoral person sins against his own body. Sin is sin, but sexual immorality means you sin against your own body?! Well…yeah! *Your body is a temple of the Holy Spirit, it belongs to God, not you. It* is bigger than just you. You should be doing all that you can to avoid sleeping around, watching porn, and having affairs. This means being careful not to purposely put yourself in predicaments where you lust after someone. When you have sex with someone, a piece of you is always with that person. That piece of you should be reserved for your other half. When you get married, the two of you become one flesh so, if you commit this sort of sin, you are certainly not alone. Since you are one flesh, the sin is now between you, your partner, and

God. That is HEAVY!

Sex is beautiful and wonderful and a true gift from God. It is meant to be shared between man and wife because of the emotion and connection that it creates. Don't confuse erotic images and fantasies with love. Don't look for your worth in the bedroom with random people. Lust is not what God intended for us. Love and sex compliment each other beautifully and should always coexist.

Say this Prayer:

Father God, help me to keep my thoughts on my husband and this marriage. Help my husband to have eyes for only me. Let us be passionate lovers and partners always. Help us to stay away from distractions and temptations and to remain a united front. Let our marriage be filled and overflowing with a love that you designed especially for us. Let our hearts never part and help our love and passion for one another to always be as fresh and as magical as it was on our wedding day. In Jesus' name I pray, amen.

19

Loving Me For Me

It is a wonderful feeling to be attracted to your spouse. Your husband of course, thinks you're beautiful. You look at your husband and swoon. There is nothing wrong with that but make sure that isn't all you see/have to offer. Your body/looks will change and so will his. What else is there? During the Coronavirus pandemic, it was reported that an unprecedented amount of couples had broken up during quarantine. These are people who had been "in love" and had been going "hot and heavy" for quite some time. Even some of the biggest "relationship goals" social media couples and celebrities were impacted. What would cause them to call it quits and, during such uncertain times?

Lots of these couples had nothing in common besides their bedroom theatrics and weren't around one another very often before the pandemic. Jobs, children, and travel meant that many would only come home to their spouses and eat dinner before going to bed, and starting over the next day. The pandemic forced people to spend quality alone time together and to *really* talk. It was then that people discovered how empty, clueless, childish, or unintelligent their spouses were. They were finally able to see the real that had been hiding under the lust. They discovered that they didn't have anything in common, didn't really like each other, and had no business being together in the first place. This is no surprise.

The problem for most people searching for their soul mate is that they aren't looking for anything real. Men and women are basing their love off of their attraction to someone. "How's the body, and what do they look like?" has replaced "Does he know God or is he a good person?" If he makes a ton of money, he must be husband material. Forget the fact that he is a womanizer. If she looks good and dances a certain way, men are all over her. What about what sort of influence she will have over your daughter one day? Will she be a true helpmate? Does she know how to pray?

A nice physical appearance, fame or money, will never sustain your marriage. When those things fade and all you've got is each other, what will you do then? Find someone who sees you for the good woman that you are. The one who doesn't care if you wear makeup, paint your nails, or shave your legs. Be with the man whom you can be your complete self with because he loves all of you, then- return the favor. Some of the most beautiful people you've ever met, were no good for you. Beauty has nothing to do with compatibility or how well someone will love you. Find out where his heart lies. Love must be sincere.

1 Samuel 16:7 "But the LORD said to Samuel...The Lord does not look at the things man looks at. Man looks at the outward appearance, but the Lord looks at the heart.'"

Say this Prayer,

Father God, send me a love that is just for me. Let him crave my mind, and caress my dark places. Let him be your gift that is just for me. Thank you for sending me someone who will see me through your eyes and love me with a powerful and unconditional love. Your timing is perfect and I thank you for allowing me to experience agape love and for wrapping us in your embrace. This love blows my mind and I thank you for it everyday. You are everything and I know that this love is your will for me. Thank you Father. In Jesus' name I pray, amen.

20

Shhh!!!Just Tell God

There will be times when you have a fight or disagreement and you need to "get it off your chest" with your family and or friends. This is harmless right? Wrong!

Gen 2:24 KJV Thy highest allegiance, except God, shall be to thy wife, not thy relatives or friends.

It is not wise to share the intimate details of your marriage with your loved ones. It often leads to more heartache in the end. When we are angry and start looking to vent to others, we say things we shouldn't say and sometimes overshare due to our emotions. We later reconcile with our spouses and move on but, this is not always true for our loved ones.

Sometimes the intimate details you share about your spouse can leave a bad taste in the mouths of others. Family and friendly gatherings can become very awkward. Your loved ones might not be ok with you forgiving your spouse. Your loved ones might harbor resentment towards him. It's not fair to any of you.

Your family and friends mean well 100% of the time. They will offer advice and suggest ways for you to "fix" your relationship based on their past experiences. They might stir the pot even more by convincing you to do things that you shouldn't do. You'll hear phrases like "If I were you...." She *isn't* you. Don't let her tell you what to do. Her past relationship that went south has nothing to do with your marriage. All men are not the same and these may be two totally different scenarios. You are essentially preparing for a war with your spouse that he isn't even equipped to fight because he doesn't even know a storm is brewing.

Don't dishonor your spouse and reveal secrets that should be kept between the two of you. It is unbecoming and certainly not God's will to speak poorly against your husband.

Talk to God. Pray and think about the whole picture. Where is the disagreement stemming from? How big of a deal is it? Can you apologize? Could either of you had said things you didn't mean? Part of being married is knowing each other well enough to know when to take things personally. Is he simply frustrated because he had a bad day at work and is snapping at you simply because you're there? It's not ok but, it does happen. Do you really believe he is out to hurt you? Are you out to hurt him? You must learn to see the best in one another, because when you see the best in one another, it's much easier to weed out his true intentions even before you've had a chance to discuss things.

If you cannot solve your problems quickly enough, and you feel that talking to God isn't helping either, you need to seek your counsel carefully. Don't talk to single people, don't talk to bitter people (you know who they are), and don't talk to anyone who won't pour in to you. Try to talk to fellow believers. Speak with your clergy, or church elders. Try to connect with people who will point you towards God and have the proper insight and life experiences to give you marital advice. Your marriage shouldn't be anyone's business but the two of you and God. If you have to involve outsiders, find God's people so that He may speak through them. Bitter and alone people should never be solicited for advice.

Speak highly of your spouse in good times and in bad. Don't ever allow anyone close to you to speak poorly about your spouse. To disrespect your spouse is to disrespect you as well. You are one. Life is already hard enough, the last thing anyone needs is disapproval from their spouses inner circle long after your issues have been worked out. Keep it to yourself.

Say this Prayer,

Father God, help me to control my emotions. Don't let me be quick to be angered. Help me to speak positively over my husband and our relationship. Show me how to keep the enemy from destroying this union. Lord, I believe that you have brought us together and that you are in control. Help me to crave more of you and less of me when times get hard. Soften my heart to my husband and soften his heart to me. Allow us to look at one another as you look at us. Control our tongues and teach us to walk in love daily.

In Jesus' name I pray, amen.

21

I Don't Like Him...Sometimes!

You ever just want to smack him? He knows exactly how to push your buttons and he gets under your skin like no one else can. You love him with everything in you but, you just don't like him today! The honeymoon phase will fade. You will have an argument/disagreement. There will come a time when you will have to say you're sorry. There will come the day that you question what you are doing with this man and seriously want to leave!

Ecclesiastes 7:8-ESV "Better is the end of a thing than its beginning, and the patient in spirit is better than the proud in spirit. Be not quick in your spirit to become angry, for anger lodges in the bosom of fools."

You must learn to communicate and how to effectively get along. During the honeymoon phase, you're all over one another and think he can do no wrong. You overlook those little imperfections until one day, you're in a screaming match. Some people enjoy the honeymoon phase and try to stay in it but I submit to you that there is a better phase to be in: the long term phase. The beginning is exciting because it's passionate and full of the unknown. The longer you have been together, the better it can become. It's the honeymoon phase on repeat! When you have a chance, ask the "veteran" couples why they don't fight like they once did. It's not because they've been together for a long time, it's because they have an unspoken understanding. They know each other. They've done the work. Marriage is work. Learning your spouse is work. You won't always like each other and that's ok. Talking *at* your spouse is <u>not</u> ok. No matter how upset you are. Even if you don't realize that you are doing it. It doesn't take a talent to be mean and being mean doesn't have to be a deliberate act. Just because you don't realize you act a certain way, doesn't excuse it.

It's ok to get mad at your spouse. Try not to stay in the anger. *Respect* is the key. Even when you have a disagreement and don't like each other, you must respect each other. Respect one another enough to speak tenderly to each other. IF you can talk about it, talk about it. Learn from it, grow from it, and try to prevent it from happening again. Remember to pick your battles. If you can't let something go, step away politely. Distract yourself with prayer and wait 24 hours before bringing it up. If it loses its sting during this time, ask yourself how big of a deal it really was. Don't sweat the small stuff. Marriage is all about the long term. Chess not checkers.

Say this prayer:

Lord, I come before you feeling misunderstood and unheard in this union. My heart is full of anger and resentment and I need your help. Lord, help me to see my husband's true intentions clearly. Help me to see his heart and the love that he has for me when we are in the midst of a fight. Help me to focus my attention on our love and your love for us instead of my emotions. I thank you for being the center of this marriage and for your continued guidance over it. Soften both of our hearts and remove this anger from our hearts. Keep us surrounded with your love and mercy. In the matchless name of Jesus I pray, amen.

22

God, Husband, Wife, Children

There have been too many memes and discussions on social media not to discuss the burning question: Who comes first in the household? Husband or children? Women are falling all over themselves to make it clear that their children come first and that since their husband is grown, he should come last. Then there are the women who feel their parents come before their husbands. This is simply incorrect from a biblical standpoint and the Bible is very clear on the correct order of the family.

1 Corinthians 11:3 ESV But I want you to understand that the head of every man is Christ, the head of a wife is her husband, and the head of Christ is God. The biblical family structure clearly states the husband is the head of the family. He is your covering and the strength of the family. You are not less important than him or "weaker" than he is, your roles are just different. The role of the head of the house is not an easy one to fill. The Bible talks about being an elder in the church and what kind of man it would take to fill the position in **1 Timothy 3:1-16**. It says that to be considered to be a leader, the man must have good reputation, have self-control and be fair. He must be able to teach. Hecannot be known as a drunk, must be non violent, not quarrelsome, or greedy. He should be married and must demonstrate faithfulness to his wife and have respectable control of his children. When the church seeks it's leadership, it seeks the best. When you seek your husband, you should be looking for the same qualities. This list of qualities is a great guide on what a husband should look like as well.

Understand that when the Bible says the man is head and you are under your husband, it doesn't mean that your children don't matter. The bond that you share and the covering that your husband provides when he properly leads his family, is the best thing for your children- it is actually putting them first. Your children will grow up seeing what a healthy relationship looks like. Your sons will learn how to be men from watching one in action and, your daughters will learn what it looks to be a wife and to have a man who can truly lead and, neither of them will settle for less. Your connection to your husband is necessary. Your children will grow up one day and start families of their own. They will leave home and base their relationships off of what they had modeled to them from your union. It is Gods plan to leave and cleave. Just as you have left the nest, so shall your children, and so did your parents. You don't stop loving your parents or put your children on the back burner because you are married. You make sure they are all nurtured and cared for but your focus is on your union and God first.

The whole family foundation is built upon you and your husband. If he is the head and he gets his direction from God, you'll all be in good hands.

Say this prayer:

Lord, Please give my husband the mind and heart to lead this family. Guide his steps and keep his mind on you so that he may have thoughts like yours. Strengthen his mind, and soften his heart. Help him to be kind and loving even in times of chaos. Silence his mind when it is racing with worry and doubt. Show him how to be a great leader, father, and husband and help me to stand in the gap for him in any way he needs it. In the matchless name of Jesus I pray, amen.

23

Lonely and Married

Sometimes you can feel unheard and unseen. He doesn't look at you the way he used to. He hasn't touched you in a while. Lately he's been a little quiet. When you try to engage him in conversation to find out what he is thinking, he says nothing is wrong. Your heart has felt so heavy. You've been feeling so alone lately and you can't even tell your husband how you feel because it'll cause an argument and create more tension. You've been secretly crying because you're overwhelmed with emotion. You miss him so much and don't know what happened between you two or how to fix it. You feel like you're drowning in loneliness. **Psalm 34:18 ESV** The Lord is near to the brokenhearted and saves the crushed in spirit.

This is the time to pray and call out to God like your marriage depends on it because it does. When you let your feelings take control, you can use poor judgment and make mistakes. Loneliness is a dangerous emotion because when you feel like you're missing something, you are more likely to lean into temptation. The enemy is always waiting in the wings to destroy you and he knows your weaknesses. When you feel neglected, the enemy will send in some handsome stranger to sweep you off of your feet by saying all of the right things, at the right time. It is easy to get caught up, don't be deceived.

Your mind will start to wonder why you are still in this loveless marriage and if it's time to get out of it because God wouldn't want you to be so unhappy. Although it is not easy being unhappy in your marriage, being unhappy is not a reason to get divorced in Gods eyes. "Therefore what God has joined together, let not man separate." **Mark 10:9** God is very clear on what the grounds for divorce are and, loneliness isn't on the list. Emotions can change just like the seasons. You don't get a "Get out of marriage" free card because your marriage isn't steamy and passionate at this moment. For better or worse right?

If you are unhappy in your marriage, there are options like prayer and counseling. You could both take a break and work on reconnecting. It can sometimes be difficult to find quality time for one another due to the demands of life. Sometimes a "staycation" or weekend away could be just what the doctor ordered. If your marriage has gotten stale, freshen it up. Spend some time getting dolled up then come home and make your husband fall for you again. Work on your marriage. You love your husband and he loves you. That is more important than any disagreement. Work it out.

Say this prayer:
Dear God, please give us the ability to always see each other as home. Let him crave my touch, mind, body, and spirit. Let the flame of our love never burn out. Lord, let us never stop laughing, kissing each other goodnight, or holding hands. Help us to always be the closest lovers and the best of friends. Lord,

bless this union and fill both of our hearts with so much love that we never know what loneliness looks like. Help our marriage to be the happiest it can be. In the matchless name of Jesus I pray, amen.

24

Choked By "What If"

What are you holding on to that you need to let go of? The hurt? The broken trust and abandonment issues? Who let you down? It is not easy for you to relinquish your full control to anyone because you have trust issues.

You have found a man. This man is kind, loving, and gentle with you. He expresses that he sees a future with you and wants you to be his wife and to carry his children. He looks at you and you melt. You can see the love he has for you in his eyes. There is a sense of belonging that you feel when you are in his presence that you have never felt before with anyone else. YOU ARE TERRIFIED.

To love means being vulnerable and open. That is a huge risk and could lead you to being hurt. You have used your past traumas and heartache to build a wall around your inner self-brick by brick. Congratulations, you are safe and no one can penetrate your walls. Bad news, no one can penetrate your walls! In order for you to experience Gods best, you will need to be able to fully feel. You will need to open your heart, mind, and spirit to this man.

What if you get hurt? What if he is no different than the others? He could abandon you. He might cheat. He might be a liar. YOU have just blocked every blessing that could be coming your way with your perceived threats. There is no actual threat. **You can be so caught up in the "what ifs" that you completely miss what is.** If this man is not the reason you have trust issues, do not make him carry another mans mistakes. Do not miss what could be the best thing that ever happened to you because you have not healed from what has happened to you.

If you do not heal your heart from whatever hurt you are holding on to, you will be alone. There is nothing wrong with being alone for a spell, and it is recommended that you spend some time alone so that you know who you are and whose you are before coming together with your husband. Permanently being alone is not what God wants for you. God wants your life to be richly filled with love and happiness. Do not create problems where there aren't any. No man likes that or wants to deal with that. Bitter is not attractive and it is not of God. Let it go so that you can step into Gods promise.

You have a man who loves and wants you. He wants to be all that you need. Let him be that for you. Don't sabotage your happiness looking for something to be wrong because you think it's too good to be true, as if you are not deserving of true love. **Proverbs 14:1** "The wise woman builds her house, but with her own hands the foolish one tears hers down. Are you going to be the wise or foolish woman?

Say this Prayer:
Lord, help me to heal my heart and my mind. Create in me a new way of thinking. Help me to discern what is good for me

so that I may know the kind of happiness you have destined for me. Help me to understand that whoever hurt me in the past was not sent by you and that it needed to happen so that I could make room for the man I've been praying for. I didn't miss out on anything because you had better for me all along. Thank you for sending me the right man, who'll help lead me closer to you and who will stand beside me all the days of my life. I give you all the honor and glory. In Jesus' name I pray, amen.

25

God's Time

Don't get so caught up in your marriage and the day to day hustle that you neglect God. God is very clear in His word about the importance of spending time in His presence. It is important to go to a quiet place and be alone with God. Life can get loud and is full of distractions. You need to get away from the noise. Even Jesus got away from everyone and went to pray alone. **Matthew 14:23 ESV** After sending them home, he went up into the hills by himself to pray. Night fell while he was there alone.

God is a shoulder and a close friend. God is waiting for you to share your concerns and triumphs with Him. He wants to hear about your hopes and fears. You can laugh or cry. Your feelings and thoughts are safe with Him. **Psalm 62:8 ESV** Trust in him at all times, O people; pour out your heart before him; God is a refuge for us.

Carve out some time for God each day. Whether it's when you're driving, in the shower, or when you get home from work. Tell God about your day. Give God thanks for the small things and the big things. Thank Him for all He has done, and everything that He will continue to do. Your time with God shouldn't always be about what you need. God loves when you acknowledge Him for who He is. God loves it when you call out to Him with a heart full of thanksgiving.

God is the ultimate friend and confidant. He is there just waiting for you to invite him into your world. He desires your friendship. There is a calm and a stillness that comes when you build a solid relationship with God. You will feel fuller and lighter. When you get closer to the Lord, He will whisper things to you to help you on your path. The closer you get to Him, the clearer His voice will become to you. Gods love and presence will keep you sane no matter what is happening in the world around you. It will strengthen you and give you peace. **Philippians 4:7 ESV** And the peace of God, which passeth all understanding, shall keep your hearts and minds through Christ Jesus.

Say this Prayer:

Lord, quiet the storm going on around me. Be my peace and my light. Calm my spirit and help me to keep our relationship strong. Keep me connected to you and reliant upon you. I need you everyday in every way. You are my peace and my savior. Continue to protect me and to guide me. In Jesus' name I pray, amen.

26

The Student

Most women spell love/romance Q-U-A-L-I-T-Y -T-I-M-E. Most men spell love/romance S-E-X.

You might like it when your husband listens to you. Maybe you love it when he helps out with the dishes and chores around the house. You might like it when he buys you nice gifts or flowers. Maybe you love to be touched and caressed and when he pays attention to you. Your husband is probably more simple. He probably likes it when you touch him, when you touch him, or when you touch him! It might sound funny but, studies have shown that men think about sex much more often than women do. Ohio State University organized a study in 2016 and the average man tallied 19 sexy thoughts per day—that comes out to about once every 1.26 hours. Lots of the participants thought about it more often than that. That's a lot of sex on the brain. Does this mean that all men are sex crazed fiends? Of course not, but it does give you something to think about.

Men are not so shallow that sex is the only thing that matters to them. They want peace and security just like any one else. They want to be listened to, they want to hear words of encouragement. Tell him that you're proud of him. Make sure he knows that you see all that he does for you and your family. Laugh with him, cry with him, be his confidant, prayer warrior, and his strongest friend. A man needs to feel like he is heard, and that he matters just as much as you do. He needs to feel needed, wanted, and desired just as much as you do. The sex is the icing on the cake for a man. Kisses and love making are a needed part of the relationship for both of you. It keeps the passionate bond alive.

Make sure he knows what matters to you. Intimacy is important to most women. If quality time is a big deal for you, make sure he knows that early on. Men are very simple and don't read minds. Don't expect him to know what you need, show him. You have to communicate both verbally and physically. Teach each other how to love each other. The learning process can be quite a rewarding experience.

It is important to teach your spouse about what matters to you. It is important that you learn what is important to your spouse. If you both know how to make each other feel loved, it's much easier to keep the stress down. When you don't feel like you are being heard or your needs are being met, it can cause a strain in your relationships. Be a lifelong student of your relationship. No matter how he presents himself and no matter who he is, study his needs. He should be doing the same. You will be a different person in your 3o's than you were in your 20's. You'll have a different outlook in your 40's than you did in your 30's. Your 50's will look very different than your 40's and so forth. At every milestone in your lives, learn and grow in love. Life is always an adventure together rediscovering who you both grow into. Enjoy the journey.

Say this Prayer:

Lord, let us pay close attention to one another. Let us always be looking for new ways to love and make each other feel special. Let us study one another. Let our love grow stronger each year. Let our bond be unbreakable. Let us be passionate and lust after only each other always. In Jesus' name I pray, amen.

27

Pasts Can Sink The Future

Our God is the master of mercy.

Isaiah 43:25 KJV "I am he who blots out your transgressions for my own sake, and I will not remember your sins". Imagine being capable of bestowing this kind of grace on someone. You're going to have to do more than imagine if you want your relationship to work. Unfortunately, human beings are not perfect. There will come a time in your relationship that you will need to forgive your spouse for something. It doesn't mean it was something as big as infidelity, broken trust is broken trust.

The past must remain in the past. You must be careful what you forgive your spouse for if you can't handle the fallout that will certainly come down the road. The past can kill any hopes for a future. You will have flashbacks and there will be times that the past comes back to haunt you in your dreams. You can't bring it up and have another fight each time you have a memory resurface. You don't get to drag your spouse through the mud and reopen old wounds whenever you see fit. Forgive and move on - as hard as it is to do.

Love means compromising and bending sometimes. You can't be moving forward while still looking back. You can't be waiting for the other shoe to drop while planning a beautiful future. It's confusing and counterproductive. Just because someone hurts you once, doesn't mean it'll happen again. Trust is full. No such thing as half trust. Either you trust or you do not.

You have been wounded and don't want to feel that sort of hurt again. It's understandable but unacceptable. If you're going to open your heart, you must open your heart. Don't live life waiting for things to go wrong. You will find yourself so distressed by the perceived threat, that you will miss out on the opportunity to be fully present and loved.

Say this Prayer,

Father God, teach me to trust again. Empty my heart of fear. Empty my heart of heartache. Guide me and lead me. Let my husband love me as you would have him to love me. Help me to overcome my pain. Fill my heart with joy and love. Help us to move on and to be stronger than ever in love and in you. You know who my husband really is and you know his true intentions. Help him to love me properly and fill him with the Holy Spirit. I surrender my heart and my marriage to you Lord.

In Jesus' name I pray, amen.

28

Leave and Cleave

B.O.U.N.D.A.R.I.E.S. Say it out loud! Boundaries. Boundaries are essential if you plan to have a healthy and happy marriage. The two of you are coming together to form a beautiful union and become one. Life as you know it is going to change- for the better hopefully. You may be someone who comes from a big beautiful family. Perhaps you have a very close knit friend circle. Maybe your husband is the social butterfly of the relationship while you are the introvert. What do you do? How do you mesh your two lives and become one without losing sight of your truths? Boundaries. Friends and family must understand that you are married now and things must change. Being married doesn't negate the fact that you love your friends and family, it simply shifts the dynamics of those relationships.

Genesis 2:24 ESV: "Therefore a man shall leave his father and his mother and hold fast to his wife, and they shall become one flesh." Rule number one: Your spouse comes first. This is God's design, don't get upset. You are no longer daughter first, sister first, friend first, or even mommy first. From a biblical standpoint, you are a wife first. Don't worry, the same applies for your hubby. He is the head of your household and your union should be his priority.

One of the biggest issues couples face is figuring out how to balance their family and friendships with their relationship. Who are your friends? What are their interests? Do they fit into who you were, or who you are now? Are all of your friends single? The issue is not that they're single, do they have a core value system in line with yours? Are they a threat to your relationship? Is your spouse comfortable with your friends? Are you comfortable with his? Why or why not? Your husband may have a friend you dislike, picture him in your mind. What is it about him that ruffles your feathers? This will be an issue down the road unless you unpack it now. There's a reason you dislike this friend, but your issue is with your man only, not his friend. Your husband must make wise decisions despite any peer pressure he may be receiving from his "boys". If he was man enough to feel that he was ready for marriage, he should be man enough to not let anyone persuade him to revert to his old "bachelor style" ways or take him out of character.

Family is family no matter what. You are bonded to them by blood. You both now have an extended family. If one of you is very family oriented and comes from a tight knit family, the other should make an effort to be close to their in laws as well. You now have an even bigger family-count your blessings. Do not allow family to shun you because you are now spending most of your free time with your spouse. With work-life balance, there aren't always enough hours in the week to spend time with your family the way you once did and those relationships can be strained. Your family may even blame your spouse. Lovingly explain to your loved ones that your priority is the family that you have created and your union comes before everything. Don't ever feel bad about putting your spouse first. Call and text your friends and family and make sure they know they still matter to you. Try to see them whenever possible, but your spouse is number one. Your loved ones will have to understand. Make no mistake, this doesn't mean you're in prison. Have girl's nights out and encourage him to have time away from you. A little time apart is good for both of you. If either of you is used to going out every night, and being the life of the party, *that* is what will need to change. You are not single anymore.

Say this prayer:

Father God, please help us to find balance in our home. Teach us patience as we transition into married life. Teach us how to walk with you. Teach us how to be a great couple, and how to maintain solid relationships with our friends and family outside of our home. Give us the compassion to love those around us and the discernment to know when people are toxic to our relationship-even friends and family. Bless us to be surrounded with people that will love, support and, pray for our union and want the best for us. In the mighty name of Jesus I pray, amen.

29

The Importance of Being Present

If you put the time in and make an effort, your relationship will blossom. There are seemingly endless distractions to keep your focus off of your husband and his focus on everything but you. Society has become such a microwave, "I want it now," ADHD, narcissistic place, that it's no wonder your focus can drift from time to time. You must make a conscientious effort to be present.

Look your husband in the eye. Share a meal together. Talk about more things than your problems. Watch movies. Laugh together. Go for long drives. Spend as much uninterrupted time together as possible. You can scroll through your social media feed, check the news, or watch tv later. When you are with your spouse, that should be all you're doing. Quality time, should be quality time. It matters. You both need to be heard and to be able to let your guard down to a partner who is available. Respect your man enough to put your phone down, turn it off, or even leave it in another room so that you're not tempted to check that notification. No one likes to be interrupted by phone calls or texts when they are trying to have a conversation or spend time with you. It's rude. You don't like it either. Treat your spouse how you want to be treated.

The enemy is out to destroy families and if we are not careful, it can easily happen. Intimacy builds trust and connection. You'd be surprised how much alone time together can keep you close. At the end of a long day when you come in from work, find your man and hug him immediately, without any words. Studies have shown that after a long day, silently embracing your spouse for at least 2 minutes can calm your brain and help stress to dissipate. Your brain will then subconsciously identify your spouse as a "Safe haven" and it will store this information. It works magic for your bond. Call your spouse during the day if you can. Voice is always better than texting because you can hear the love and the smile in their tone and it's nice to be reminded that you're on each other's minds.

Staying grounded in your faith and in one another will help to fend off the enemy. Your union will withstand the test of time if you remember to stay close and to enjoy one another as often as possible. Get dressed up, go on dates, hold hands, and never stop kissing each other. The "lonelys" will never penetrate a happy heart because a happy heart is so full of love, there is no space for lonely or neglect.

13. 1 Peter 5:8 ESV Be sober, be vigilant; because your adversary the devil, as a roaring lion, walketh about, seeking whom he may devour. Make the decision together in the beginning that your marriage will not be on the chopping block and that you will not leave the door open for the enemy to walk in.

It is easy to be tempted by the noise that is going on around you. Be vigilant and be aware. You will be tempted, you will be distracted. Turn your eyes back on the Lord and your husband

and the Lord will give you a way out. Temptation is a part of life but it doesn't have to overtake you. **1 Corinthians 10:13** No temptation has overtaken you that is unusual for human beings. But God is faithful, and he will not allow you to be tempted beyond your strength. Instead, along with the temptation he will also provide a way out, so that you may be able to endure it.

Marriage is not rocket science. Don't lose your bond or your connection to one another. Make an effort for your spouse and he will make an effort for you. Never stop dating, never stop loving, and never stop putting each other first. Let your love be your biggest distraction.

Say this prayer:

Father God, please be a fence around this marriage. Let us never lose sight of our love. Let us remain the closest of friends and always each other's top priority. Let his arms always be a safe haven for me. Let me never stop being his peace and his home. Let us cherish our friendship and our connection. Lord. when we lose our way, please bring us back to you and each other. In Jesus' name I pray, amen.

30

Forgiveness

For-give. verb
Stop feeling angry or resentful toward (someone) for an
offense, flaw, or mistake.
Merriam Webster

Since no one is around we can be honest with each other. What
has your husband done that you told him you'd forgiven him
for but, you secretly haven't let it go yet? As women, once we
get hurt, we forgive and try to move on but, we have difficulty
building trust again. This is especially true when the hurt comes
unexpectedly from the men we have chosen to love. We love
them enough to stay with them through our hurt but we carry
their indiscretion with us like a get out of jail free card, just
waiting to flash our pass whenever we feel cornered. This is
wrong!

Forgiveness, true forgiveness, is not bringing up the issue
again and allowing yourself to move on completely. This is one
of the hardest things in the world to do. It's not because you've
been hurt, you have trouble fully moving on because you fear

it may happen again. It's a defense mechanism. You are never going to see your marriage reach it's full potential as long as you do this. What you are doing is literally the equivalent of pulling off a scab. The skin gets damaged, a blood clot forms to protect it, new tissue generates, and before your skin can be revealed good as new, you pull the scab off and the healing process has to begin again- how counterproductive.

Ladies, be honest with your men. You can't choose both. You either forgive him or you don't. If a man truly loves you and hurts you, it also hurts him every time he is reminded of what he did. Each time you look back and dredge it up, you are robbing both of you from the present. Don't tell him you forgive him if you honestly don't.

A great bible verse about forgiveness is **Proverbs 17.9ESV** - He who conceals a transgression seeks love, But he who *repeats* a matter separates intimate friends. This means that you and your husband are friends. Keeping the transgression covered is you acting out of love. It is love and a loyalty to our partner that keeps us from repeating mistakes. We choose to forgive and set things aside rather than bringing up the sin again. This kind of forgiveness allows us to be whole and shields our husbands from having to constantly bear the guilt and relive whatever pain they've caused us. The text goes on to say that he who *repeats* a matter separates intimate friends. What does that mean? This simply means that now that the issue has been brought up and you've dealt with it, it is over - and cannot be brought up again - even when you get mad! Don't keep reminding him over and over again of his mistake. Forgive and move on because if you don't, you will destroy your friendship.

You must choose your battles wisely. If your husband has acknowledged his mistake and you have forgiven him, you owe it to the both of you to invest your full heart- devoid of resentment.

Say this prayer:

Father God, I come before you hurt and afraid because of things that have happened in my marriage. I ask that you touch the heart of my husband and give him a mind to be more like you. God I ask that you heal my heart and allow me to see my husband as I did before the hurt. God I ask that you take this unforgiveness out of my heart and out of my mind so that our marriage can grow and reach it's fullest potential. God, please be the center in this marriage and teach us to trust in you. In the mighty name of Jesus I pray, amen.

31

That's Marriage

Marriage is a beautiful blessing from God and it is close to His heart. When a man finds a wife, he finds a good thing. As you embark on a lifetime of love together, always put God and your union first. There'll be hard days. Days you spend on your knees in despair. There'll be days of laughter and of celebration. Sometimes you'll be sure of everything and, somedays you won't have a clue about anything.

Your patience will be tested as much as your faith. You will be there for every joy and every piece of bad news. You will be an anchor and a rock. Selfless, generous, and compassionate.

Sometimes you will feel unheard and you will have days that you contemplate leaving for good- and you'll come back. No matter what may come your way, marriage is a beautiful journey through life sharing one heartbeat. It is meant to last forever and it truly is a blessing.

Take the hand of your King and husband and no matter what happens in your lives, never let it go. As long as you keep God with you and you never lose sight of the love you share, you will find success on journey.

Here's to your forever happily ever ever after. May you share the kind of love that awakens the soul and is so solid, that you know that only God could have sent it. May you wake up everyday with joy in your heart and the kind of relationship that you've always dreamt about. I am praying for Gods best for you and your family. God loves you and so do I.

My prayer:

Father God, let the beautiful woman of God reading this have a heart that is full and a life that she treasures. Give her all of the desires of her heart and allow her to be a blessing to many. Let the love her husband showers her with be her constant reminder of your authenticity and your eternal love for her. Let her soul never be weary. Put a smile on her face but let the smile in her heart be even bigger. I pray for joy and abundance over this womans' life Lord. Bless her and everyone connected to her. I thank you and give you the praise in advance because I know it is already done. In the mighty name of Jesus I pray, amen.

32

Your Notes And Thoughts....

About the Author

Shaleea Venney is a 3 time bestselling Author, Speaker, Blogger, and Podcast Host. Once a teen mom, it has been her mission to show other young women how to overcome their environments and circumstances. She has been with her husband since they were teenagers. They have been together for 18 years and celebrated 10 years of marriage in 2020. Together they are the parents of two teenagers- one boy, and one girl. Shaleea and her family live in California.

You can connect with me on:
🌐 https://www.shaleeavenney.com

Subscribe to my newsletter:

✉ https://www.shaleeavenney.com/home

www.ingramcontent.com/pod-product-compliance
Lightning Source LLC
Chambersburg PA
CBHW031521040426
42445CB00009B/337